"The Twelve Days of Christmas"

By Elizabeth Jancewicz

Dedicated to
NormaJean, Bill, Gudrun, and Daryl

"A partridge in a pear tree."

It's debated whether this carol originated from England or France. Since the version I know is in English, I chose to base my illustrations on British flora, fauna, and 16th century culture. Therefore, this first illustration depicts a female grey partridge (also known as the English partridge) nesting in a Conference pear tree, a pear variety developed in Britain. And for fun, I made sure to hang 12 pears in the branches, as a nod to the song as a whole.

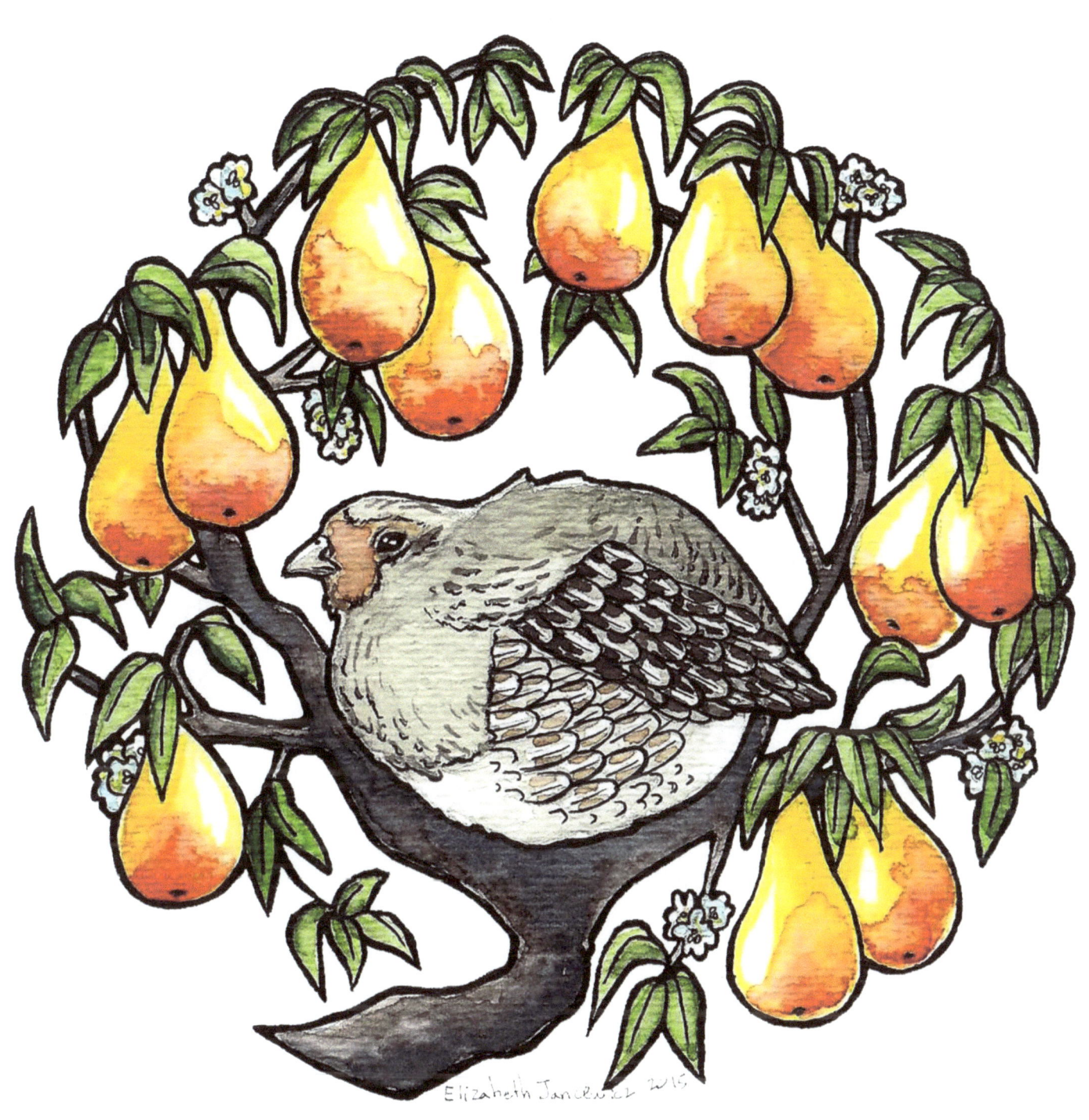
Elizabeth Janclewicz 2015

"Two turtle doves"

The turtle dove (more specifically the European turtle dove) is smaller than most doves and distinguishable from other doves and pigeons by its smaller size, black and white striped patch on the side of its neck, and vibrant wing markings when in flight. The surrounding branches are from the Norway spruce, considered the "original Christmas tree". Again, 12 spruce cones nod to the title of the carol.

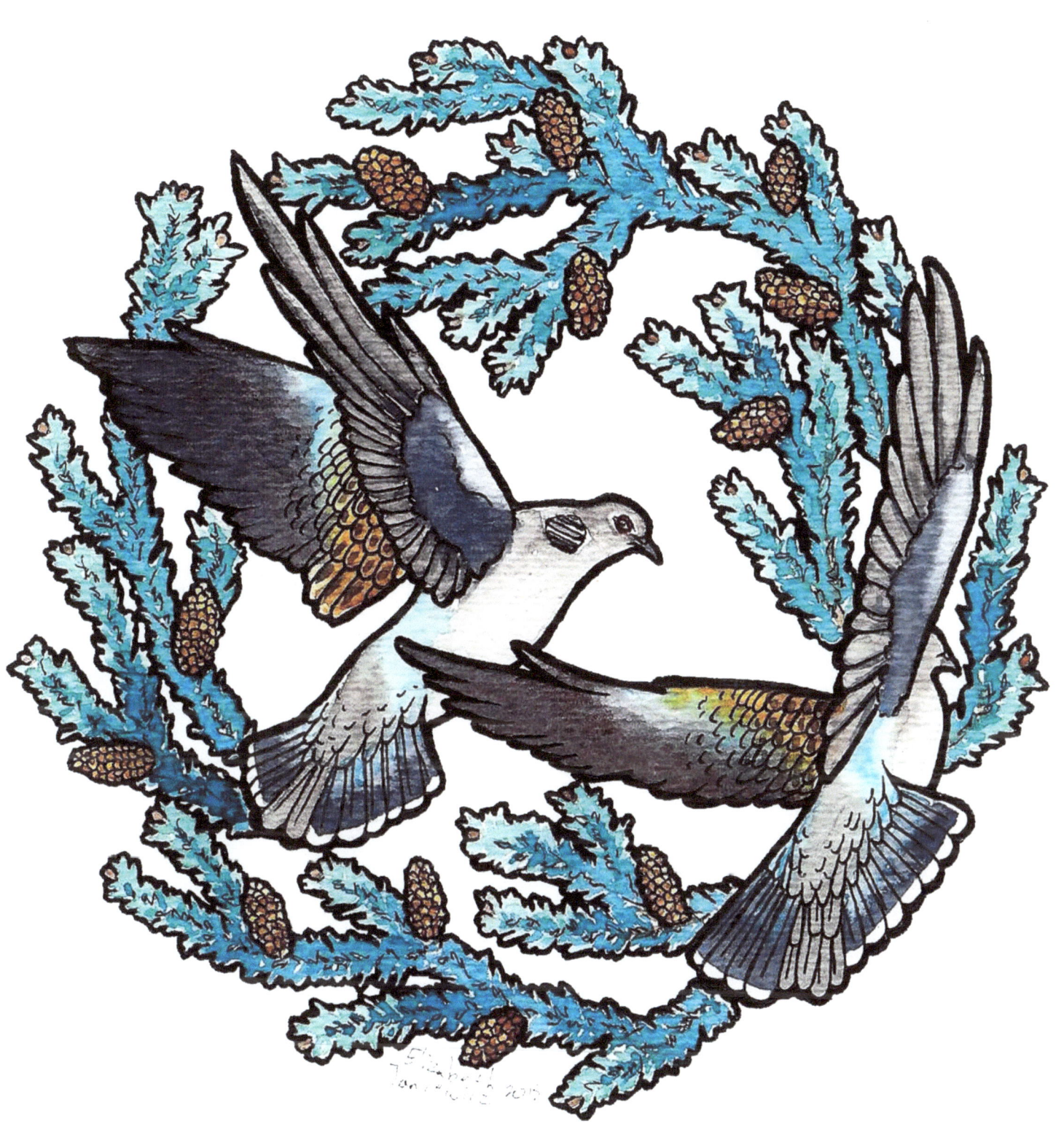

"Three French hens"

One of the main reasons I chose to view this carol with the focus on British culture is because the third day is the only one that specifically mentions that the gift is French. (If the song was sung in France, why would this be pointed out?) This illustration features three Faverolle hens, a specifically French breed of chicken. Along with irises, the national flower of France.

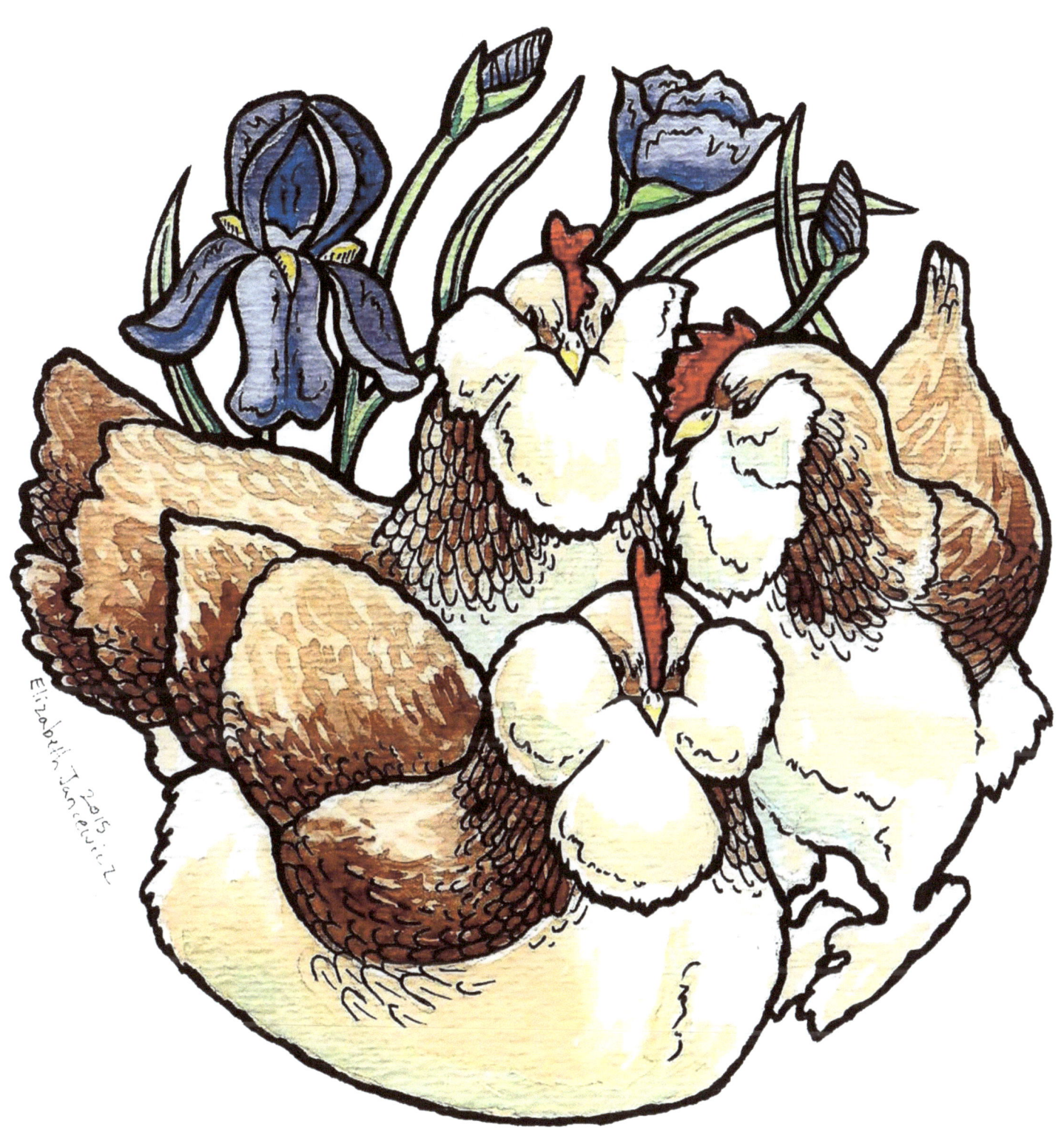

"Four Calling Birds"

The earliest known version of this carol, from the 16th century, refers to the fourth gift as "four colly birds", colly being a regional English expression for the word "black". Solidifying the gift as "calling birds" didn't happen until the early 20th century. Therefore, I chose to depict the fourth illustration with the common European blackbird.

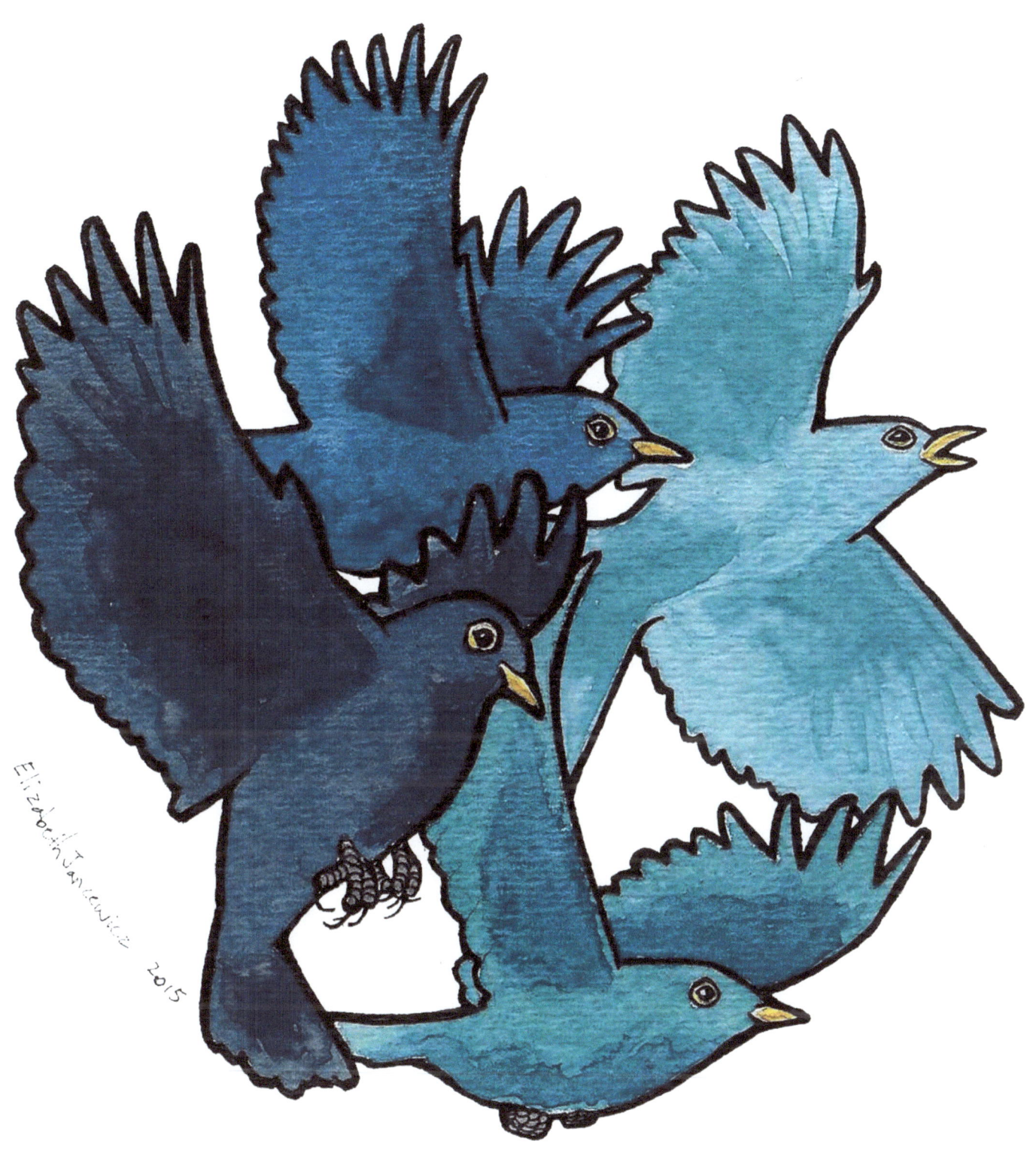

"Five gold rings"

Firstly, saying "golden" rings seems to be a recent edit, and used primarily in North America, so I'm sticking with the traditional and European "gold" rings.
As for the illustration, I had been dreading this gift since I began this illustration series. I prefer painting subjects that hold my interest, and the thought of painting five plain gold rings seemed so incredibly dull. But then I found that quite a few historians believe that the first seven gifts of this carol are all birds, and that the five gold rings could actually refer to the gold and black coloured cape beneath the eye of the male ringed or Chinese pheasant. The striped pattern of the feathers can look like five gold rings.

There are a few other options for what the five gold rings refers to, but this one seemed the most interesting to me.

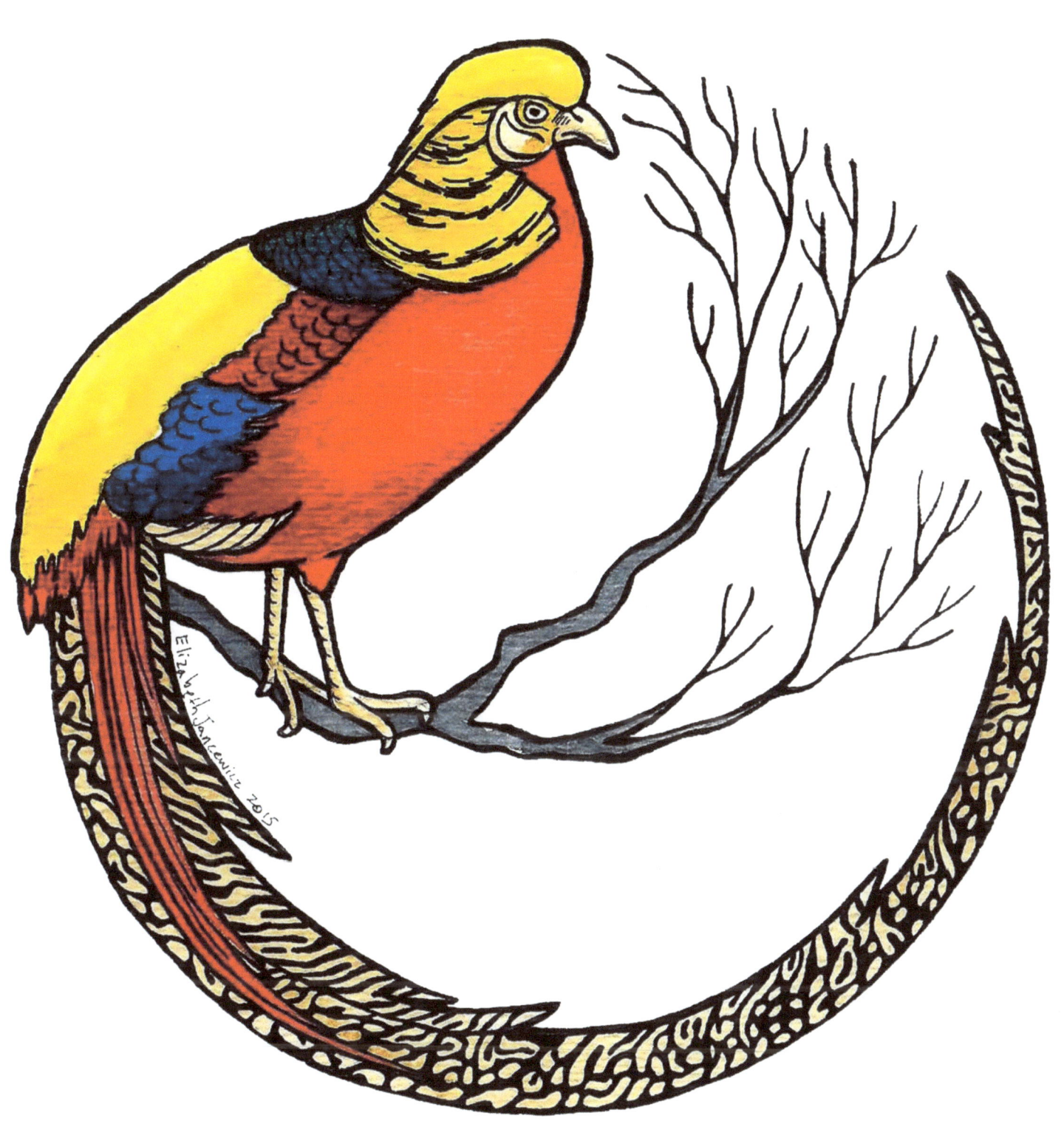

"Six geese a-laying"

The greylag goose is thought to be the only goose species specifically native to Britain. I chose to illustrate the greylag goose because they usually mate for life, and while the female does the actual incubation, the male usually stays very close to the nest. Once the eggs hatch, the care of the young geese is shared evenly between both parents. I figured it would be appropriate therefore to show three female and three male geese, as they all participate in the "laying".

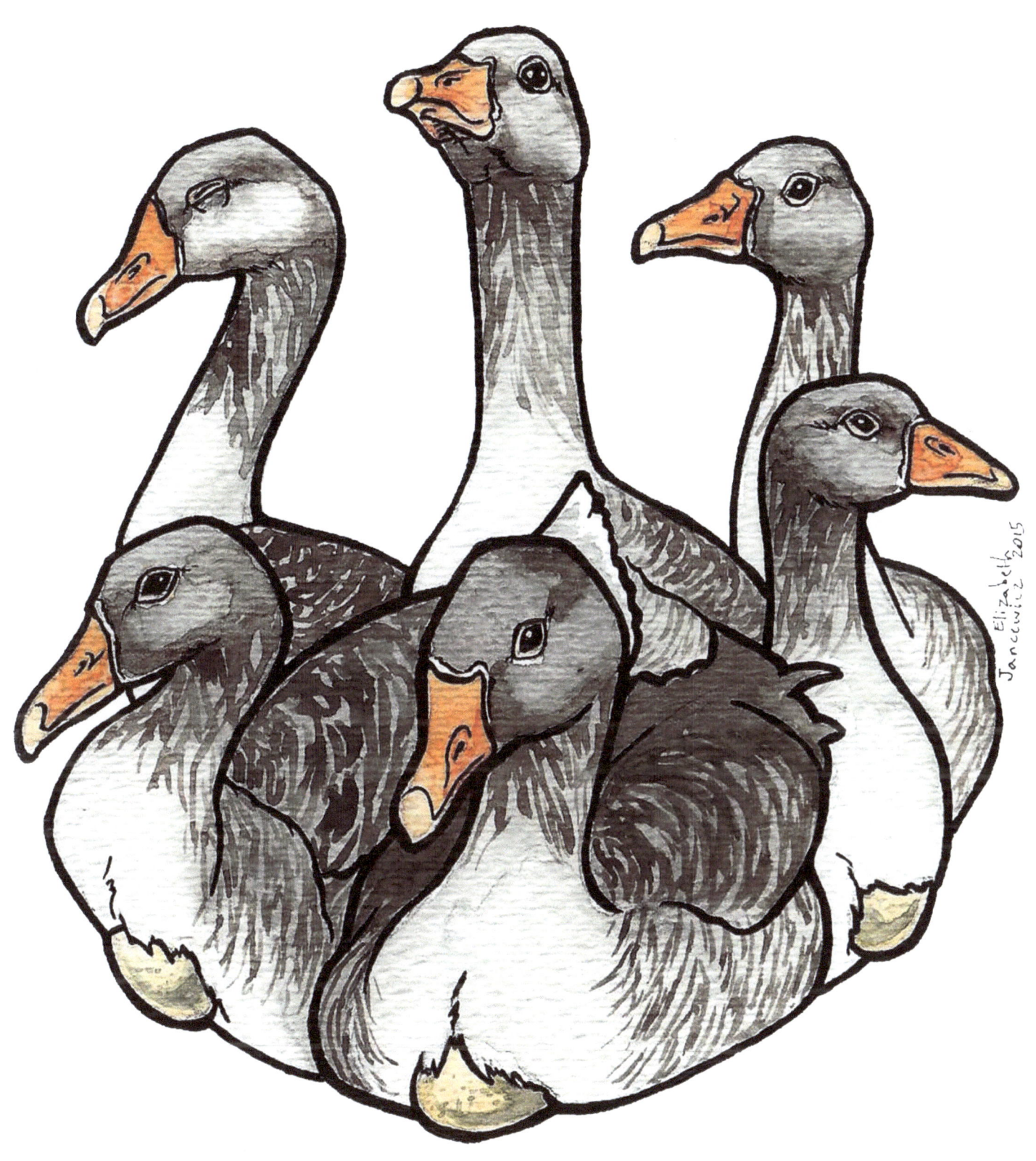

"Seven swans a-swimming"

The mute swan is identified by its mostly white body, orange bill bordered in black with a pronounced knob atop the bill, and it being less vocal than other swan species. Dating back to the 12th century, the British monarchy has claimed ownership of all unmarked mute swans, causing them to be known as the "Royal Bird". To this day, a census of mute swans is performed yearly for the Queen.

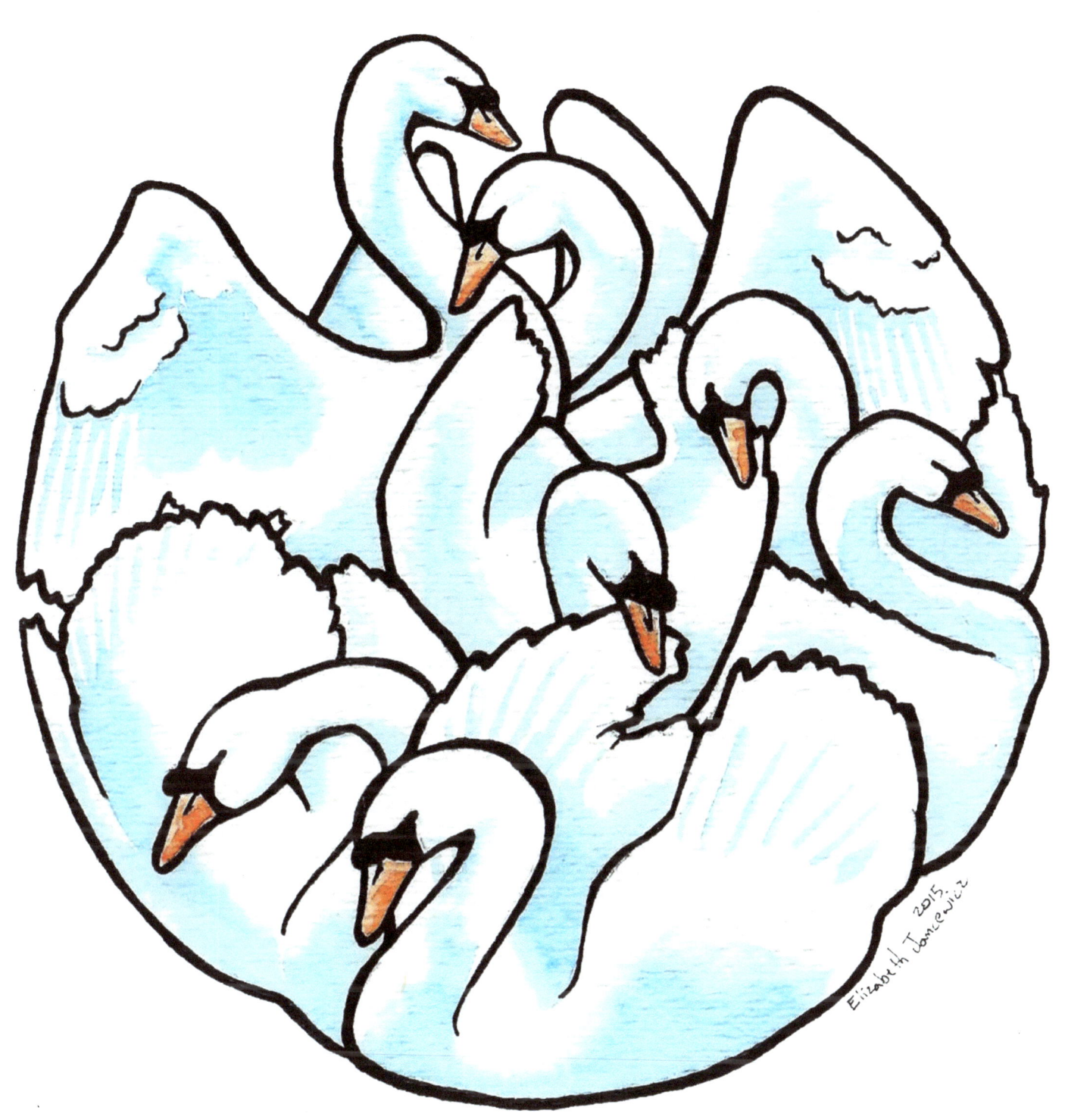

"Eight maids a-milking"

For the costumes on the eight maids, I referred to 16th century paintings of common peasant women in England. The cow peering out from behind the maids is a Dairy Shorthorn, the oldest pedigree-registered breed of cattle in the world, with records of being used for milk dating back to the 16th century in England.

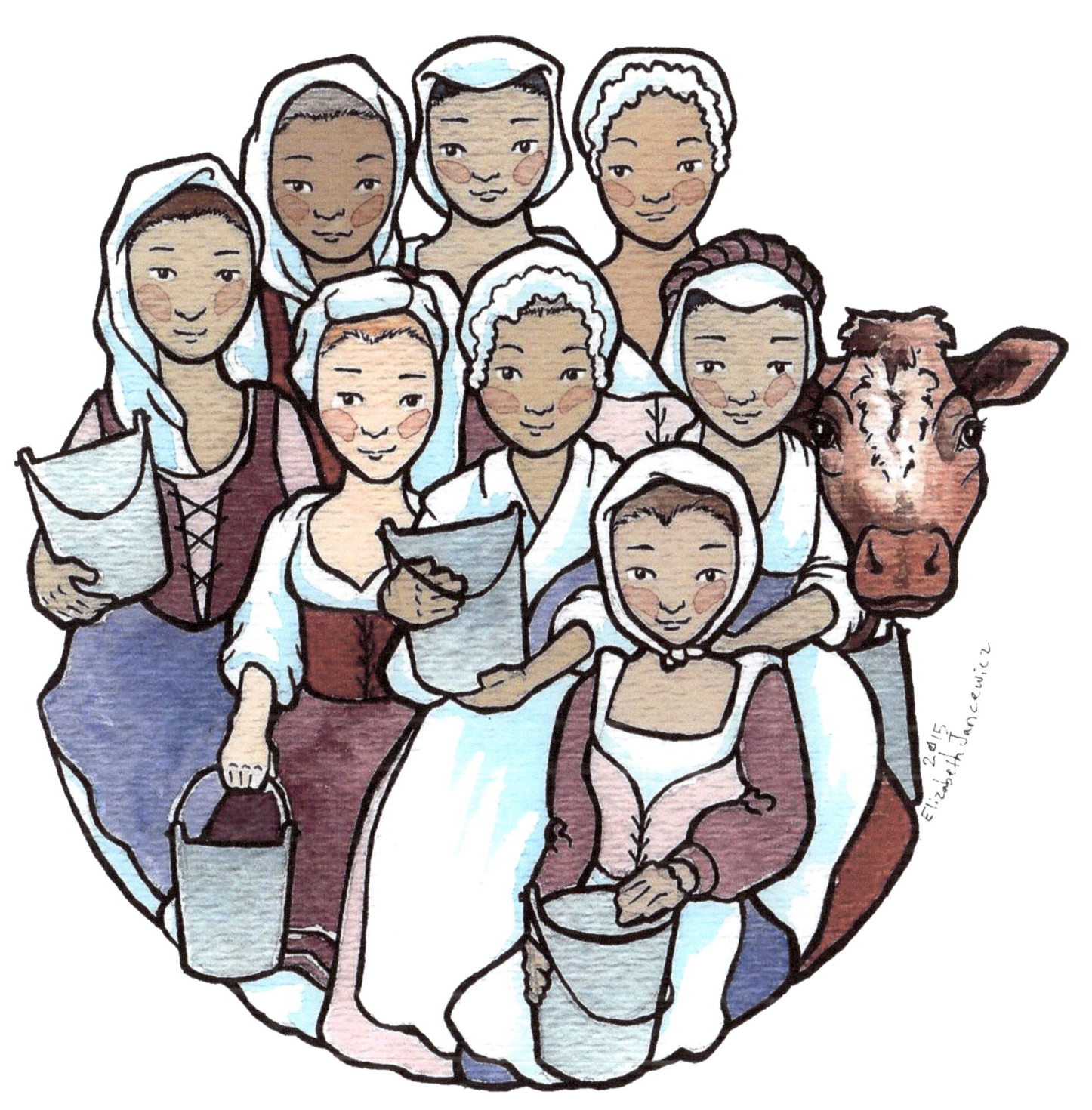

"Nine ladies dancing"

As with the 8th gift, for the 9th I looked at paintings of women from the 16th century for their dresses, hairstyles, and headwear. These women are of a slightly higher class than the milk maids, so the colour and pattern of their clothing is more uniformed. The dance that they're participating in is nothing specific; perhaps a basic line dance. I really just chose this one because it was the easiest for fitting nine active ladies into a small circular illustration.

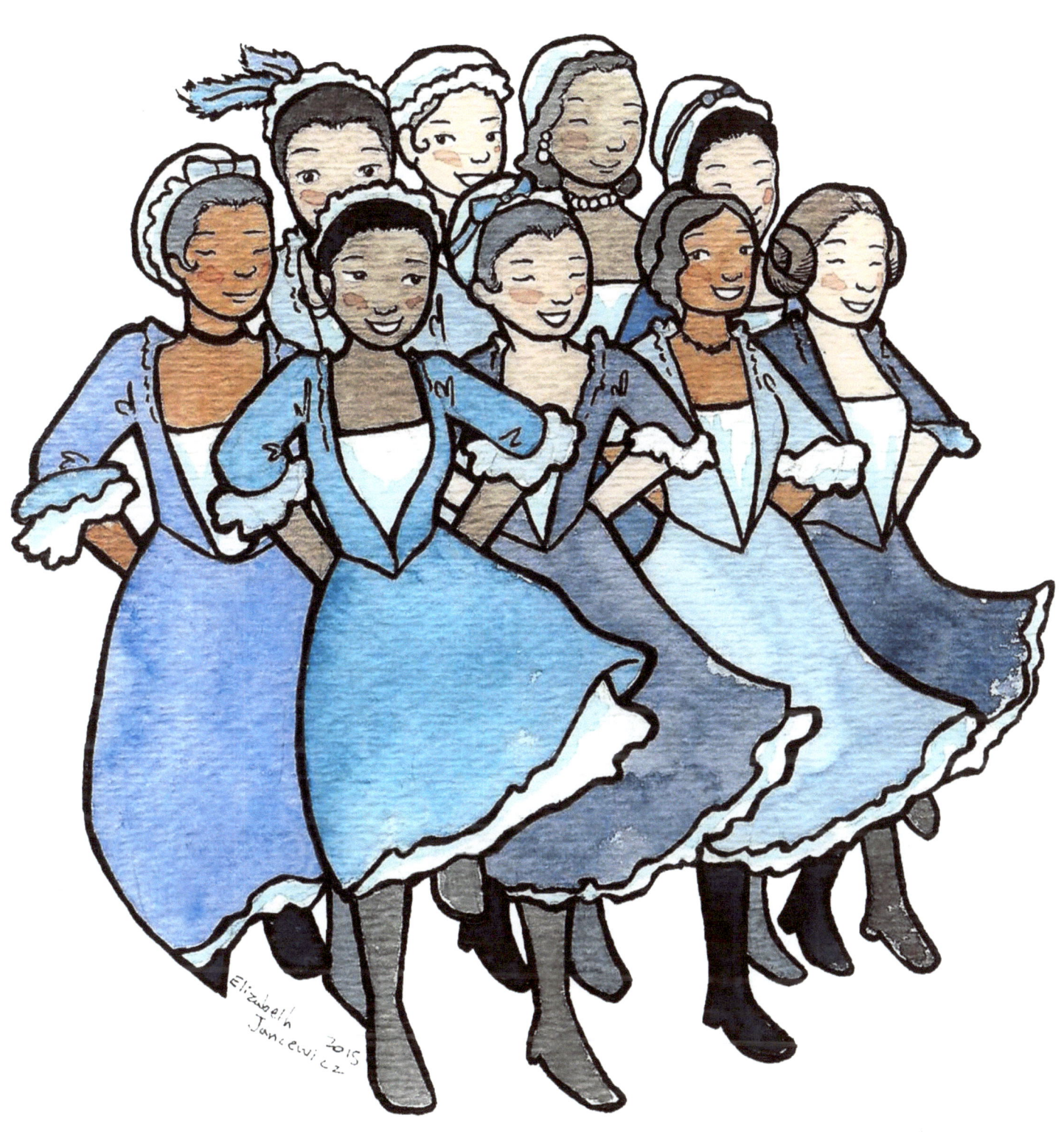

"Ten lords a-leaping"

I decided to base this illustration on classic portrait paintings of ten actual lords from the 16th century, and their leap based on the jeté, a classic ballet leap. The lords are as follows:

Front row, left to right: Thomas Wolsey, Stephen Gardiner, Sir Christopher Hatton, The Lord Henry Wriothesley, Thomas Goodrich.

Back row, left to right: Sir Thomas Audley, Sir Thomas More, Sir Nicholas Bacon, Nicholas Heath, Sir Thomas Bromley.

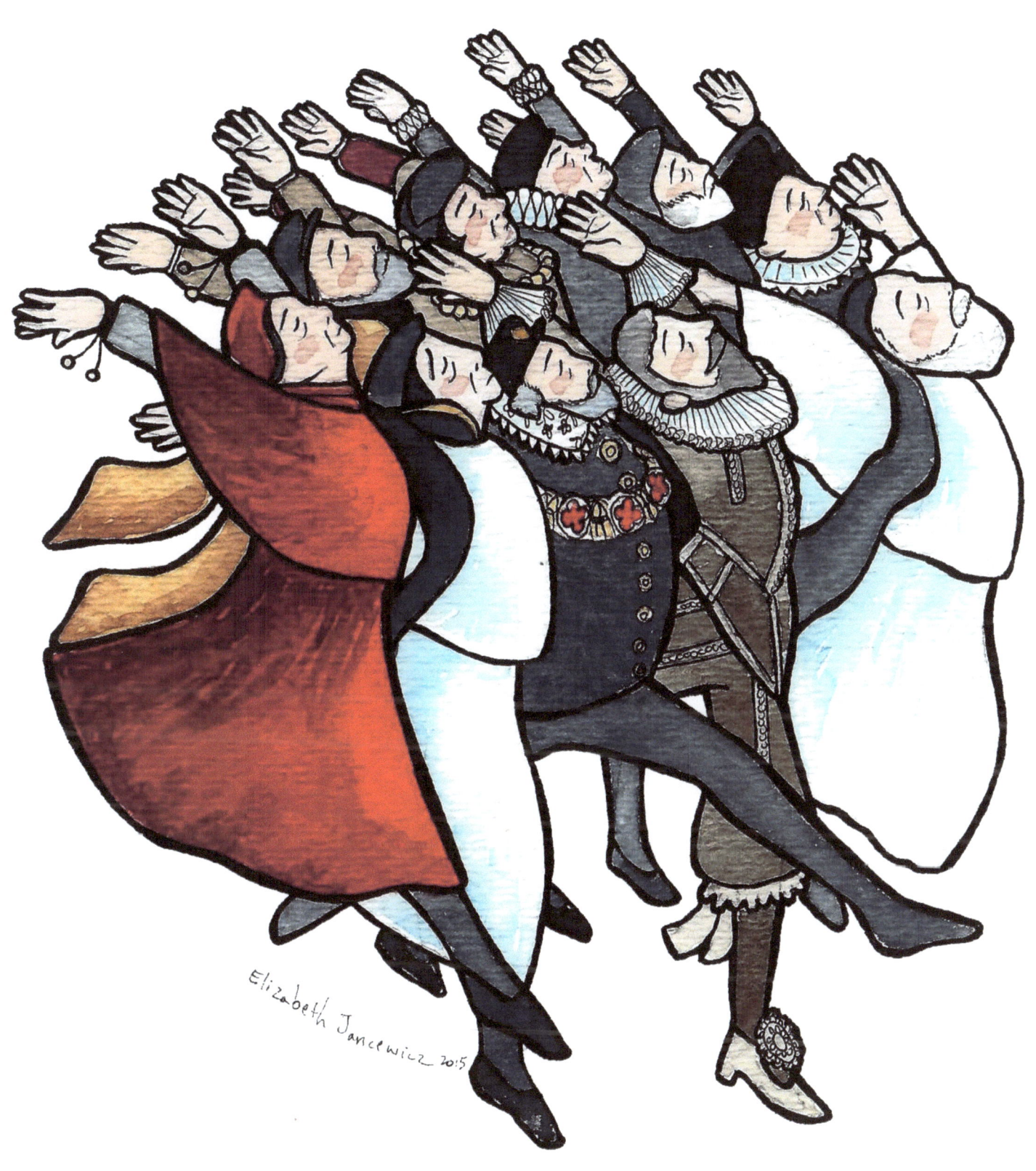

Elizabeth Jancewicz 2015

"Eleven Pipers Piping"

I was surprised to to discover that "pipers" in the 16th century refereed to bagpipers, probably because I've seen this gift usually illustrated as flutes or recorders. Once I decided to illustrate eleven bagpipers, I was able to find lots of paintings and sketches from the 16th century of individuals playing a simplified English version of bagpipes, and was also surprised to discover that the majority of the people in these paintings were women.

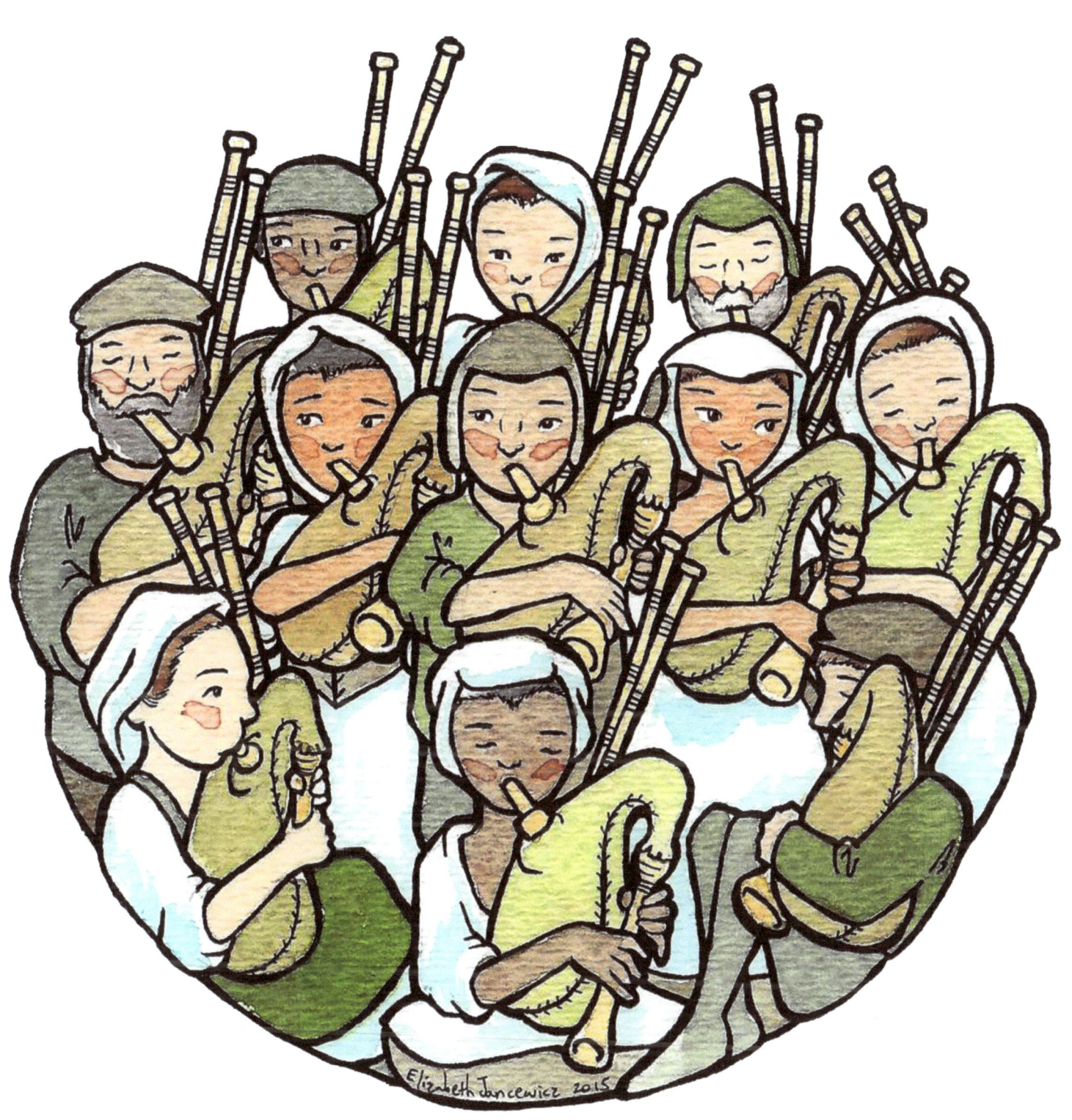

"Twelve drummers drumming"

I illustrated rope tension drums for this gift, finding this to be a fairly common drum used in the 16th century. The toughest part was looking at dozens of photos of hands holding drumsticks.

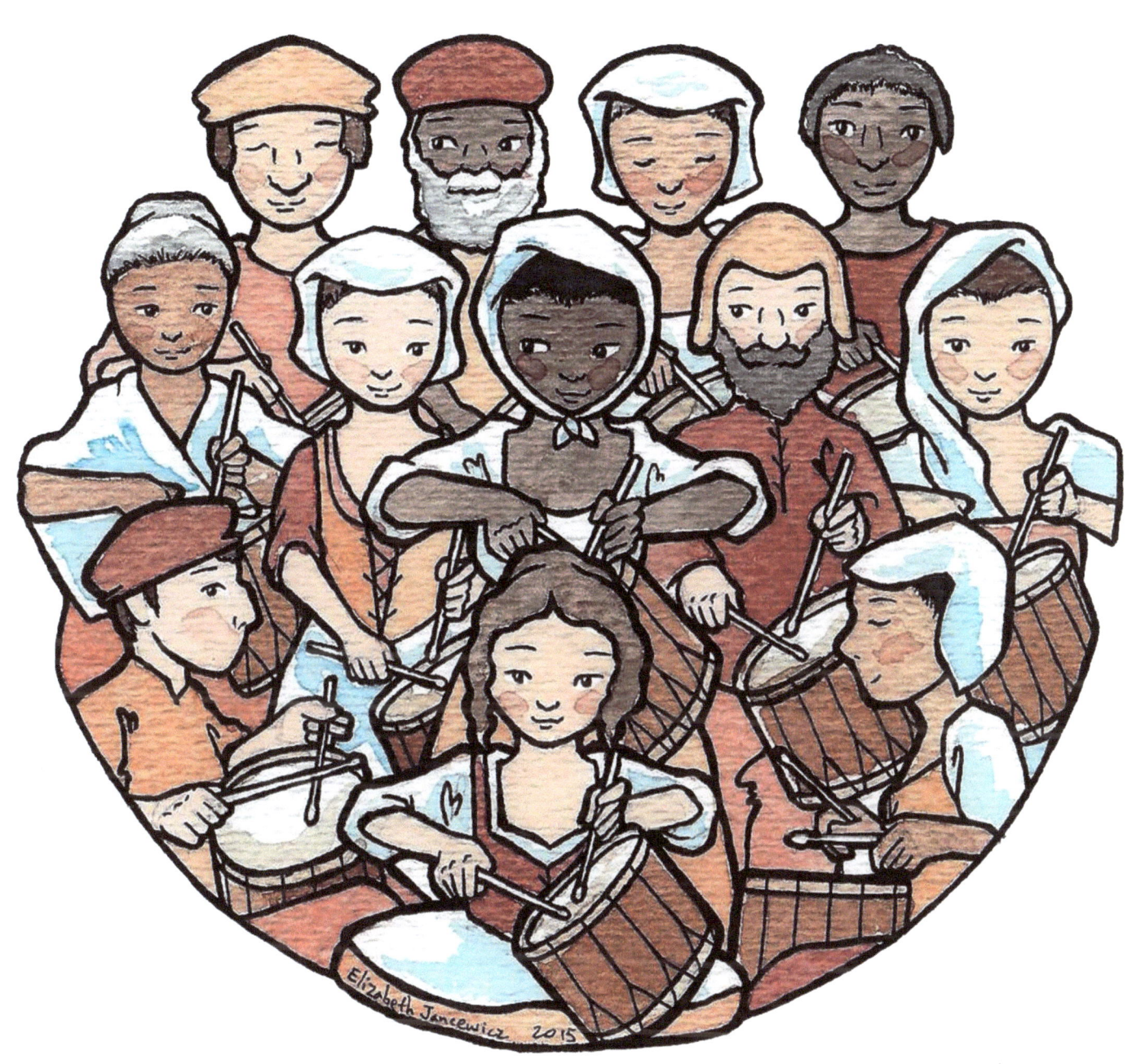